# Find a High-Paying Medical Job:

## *Building a Secure Career in Medicine*

### *By Michael LeFan*

www.highpayingmedicaljob.com
For more help see page 88

## Legal Notice

All attempts have been made to verify the information presented in this publication; however, neither the author nor publisher assumes any responsibility for errors, omissions or conflicting interpretation of the materials herein. This publication is not intended to be used as a source of legal, educational, or professional career counseling. The information in this publication may be subject to varying state or local laws or regulations that may apply to the user's particular practice. The purchaser or reader of this publication assumes responsibility for the application of this information. Adherence to all applicable laws and regulations — federal, state, and local — governing professional licensing, business practices, advertising, and other aspects of doing business in the U.S. or any other jurisdiction is the sole responsibility of the purchaser or reader. The Author assumes no responsibility or liability whatsoever on behalf of any purchaser or reader of this publication. Any perceived slights of specific people or organizations is unintentional and purely coincidental.

# Contents

Chapter One:
The Benefits of a Career in the Medical Field .............................. 6
   Health Care Jobs ..................................................... 10
   Building the Foundations of Your Career in a Medical College
   ............................................................................... 10
An Overview of Medical Careers............................................... 13
   Health Care Jobs, Medical Jobs, Hospital Jobs, Nursing Jobs . 13
   From Doctors to Phlebotomists............................................. 14
   The World of Dentistry...................................................... 16
   The World of Chiropractic.................................................. 17
   Career Medical Training...................................................... 17
   See Anything You Like?...................................................... 20
Descriptions of Medical-Related Jobs ....................................... 23
   Medical Assistant............................................................... 24
   Build a Career as a Medical Assistant ................................... 25
   Are you cut out to be a medical assistant? ............................. 26
   What does a medical assistant do? ....................................... 27
   Surgical Technologist.......................................................... 28
   Certified Nursing Assistant.................................................. 29
Dental Assistants..................................................................... 31
Office Jobs in Medical-Related Fields ....................................... 44
   What Is Medical Billing & Coding?....................................... 44
   Medical coding has never been hotter ................................... 45
   What About Professional Certification? ................................. 45
   Is Continuing Education Needed for a Career in Medical
   Coding? ............................................................................ 46
   What Skills Do You Need?................................................... 47
   Medical Billing Training and Education................................. 47
   Typical Subjects for Medical Billing & Coding Students........ 48
   Medical Billing .................................................................. 51
   Where Do You Work?......................................................... 51
   Medical Billing Employment Figures.................................... 54

Average Medical Coder Salaries (2006)..................................... 54
Finding the Right Billing & Coding Program ......................... 56
Medical Transcription ................................................................ 57
What Does a Transcriptionist Do?.......................................... 57
What It Takes to be a Transcriptionist.................................... 58
Pay Scale ................................................................................ 59
Careers in medical sales .............................................................. 60
Medical Device Careers........................................................... 60
What Would You Sell?............................................................. 63
Medical Sales Opportunities Abound...................................... 67
Durable Medical Equipment ................................................... 67
Pharmaceutical Sales.................................................................... 69
Needed Skills .......................................................................... 70
Pharmacy Technician ................................................................... 72
What You'll Study in Pharmacy Technician Courses .............. 73
Why Get Certified as a Pharmacy Technician?....................... 74
Certification Requirements ...................................................... 75
Pharmacy Technician Salaries ................................................. 76
Salary Range (as reported by Salary.com) .............................. 77
Factors Affecting Pharmacy Technician Salaries.................... 77
Pharmacy Technician Salary Benefits ..................................... 78
Medical Imaging Careers............................................................... 79
Medical Imaging Glossary....................................................... 80
Radiologic Technologist........................................................... 80
Ultrasound Techs .................................................................... 81
Ultrasound Technologist Salaries............................................. 81
Medical Imaging Salaries ........................................................ 84
Radiologic Technologists Salaries........................................... 84
Typical Salary for a Radiology Tech ....................................... 84
Cardiovascular Technologists Salaries .................................... 85
Nuclear Medicine Technologists Salaries................................ 85
Radiation Therapist Salaries .................................................... 85
Related Careers ....................................................................... 85
Radiologic Technology Jobs and Career Outlook ................... 86
For More Information.................................................................... 88
Associations and Professional Societies ....................................... 94

*Chapter One*

# The Benefits of a Career in the Medical Field

Healthcare Workers in many areas of the healthcare industry hold good jobs with only a high school diploma (or higher). They pull down average annual earnings beginning at $19,178.

You've heard it before, healthcare is "where it's at" in the job market. From home care aides, a sector expected to grow 50 percent by 2018, to nurses and pharmacy technicians, healthcare jobs are on the rise. If you only have a high school diploma, consider starting as a home care aide at an average rate of $9.22 an hour—a place you can get your foot in the door with little or no experience. Many colleges, community colleges, and vocational programs can train you as a radiologic technician or other healthcare specialist that will greatly increase your earning power.

A career in the medical field is one of the best options available for many people these days because of job security, possible career advancement, and other intangible factors. These careers also deliver job satisfaction. Obviously, there are training requirements and certifications needed before you will be eligible for a career in the medical field. Fortunately, there are some shortcuts in acquiring the training and completing the certification examinations you need. These require varying lengths of time to prepare you for the field you choose.

www.highpayingmedicaljob.com
For more help see page 88

Do not allow the need for training and certification deter you from pursuing a career in the healthcare industry. Whatever time, effort, and resources you invest in training and certification will be well worth it. Do not worry about not being able to strike quickly while the job boom in the industry is hot. You may be concerned because you cannot go right to work in healthcare until you have completed necessary training, which could take as long as two years to complete.

Not to worry; the experts say that healthcare will continue as a growth industry for years to come. That leaves plenty of time for you to prepare for and acquire a good job in one of the various fields of medicine and to build the career you are wanting.

Whether you decide to become a certified nursing assistant, a nurse, a medical assistant, a medical supply sales specialist, a laboratory technician, a medical records transcriber, or something else, many promising opportunities will present themselves to you after you have completed training and certification. Just remain diligent, determined, and passionate about your chosen path and the bright future awaiting you.

Before deciding which career you want to build in the medical world, make sure that you are facing all the facts. Do not make your decision based on what you have heard or what sounds like "fun" to you. Do your homework. Familiarize yourself with everything that your choice will require of you. This way, you will not find yourself in the middle of training and wanting to bail out because you have realized that your interests lie elsewhere.

Wherever your interests, skills, and inclinations lie, there is bound to be a medical job for which you are suited. It is vital that you find the right fit in this regard because when you enjoy what you do you will willingly give more of yourself to the work The chances of unhappy job burnout will be few or non-existent.

Fortunately, opportunities in the medical field are varied enough to accommodate individuals with many different interests and abilities. For example, if you have no previous medical training but know that you want to take advantage of choosing a career in healthcare, then all you have to do is think about your personal strengths, existing life experiences, and applicable skill sets at this point in time.

An extravert possessing excellent communication skills can choose a career such as a medical supply sales specialist, or even as a medical assistant, depending on their preferences.

## Health Care Jobs

The majority (75% or more) of health care job vacancies never make it to the classified ads. You must identify viable healthcare job opportunities through online listings, associations, directories, job fairs, job hotlines, and corporations. Also, visit the occupational listings for a sampling of the 1400+ healthcare job hunting resources listed in Health Care Job Explosion. Alternative hiring resources offer a wide variety of career possibilities. This site lists currently available jobs on its Jobs Board, key job resources for specific occupations, and recruiting sites where you will find thousands of listings. Search all sources to locate jobs in your area and specialty.

Just make sure that you take into consideration all that is needed to make the choice that is right for you.

Building the Foundations of Your Career in a

## Medical College

An individual begins a career as a doctor in medical school, while a person wanting to get into the fast growing and promising healthcare field builds the foundations of his or her career in medical-related education. Many community colleges and specialty training schools provide these types of courses within a shorter timeframe than a university — and at less cost.

Because of our aging population and technologically advanced society, the demand for excellent healthcare services is increasing. Experts say that this trend will continue for several years. With it comes the proportional increase in opportunities for employment in the medical field.

Students fresh out of high school and persons with current careers outside the medical path can realistically contemplate the investment of time and resources in medical training in order to acquire the qualifying credentials for a rewarding career in healthcare.

To get into popular medical careers such as those of medical encoding, medical billing, medical assistant, lab technician, pharmacy assistant, and medical supply sales, you must receive proper training and pass the examination for certification. Many of the most promising employment opportunities will require certified individuals to prove their competency and credentials for the job.

Since this is the case, be sure to check whether the medical college, trade school, or community college that you plan to attend offers certification courses. Or at least determine whether they will, in fact, properly train you for certification by the certifying authority. Otherwise, your time and effort may be wasted. You can check out the different medical training institutions in your area through their websites. Some offer classes online.

Make sure you explore the websites of each medical college, trade school, and community college in your area, and understand the different programs they offer as well as the reputation of their training. A reputable school will look better on your resume.

*Chapter Two*

# An Overview of Medical Careers

## Health Care Jobs, Medical Jobs, Hospital Jobs, Nursing Jobs

The medical field is one of today's fastest growing job sectors and experts predict that this trend may continue to hold true for several years to come. This means that there is a strong demand for men and women to fill these jobs. Below are a few generalized job descriptions for some medical careers. They will introduce to a few broad areas of employment in the healthcare field, and they may provide guidance to you when you are looking to launch your medical career in this growing and stable area of work.

## From Doctors to Phlebotomists

Doctors and nurses, regardless of their specialties, are in the business of relieving suffering and saving lives. Each one of them has a responsibility to the patients. To give you a better understanding of some of these positions, here are a few medical career descriptions.

When there is an emergency and you need medical attention quickly, you have to dial 911 and wait until the paramedics arrive. Another name for them is EMT or emergency medical technician. Their job is to stabilize the patient until the ambulance reaches the hospital. EMTs are the front line troops of medical care.

Once the EMT team gets the patient to the hospital, the EMTs turn them over to the emergency room doctor that will soon be assisted by other doctors, nurses, and technicians. The nurse is there to monitor the patient's condition when the physician is not around and to administer medication when instructed to do so by a physician. Aside from working in a hospital, nurses may work in a residential home, in specialized units, schools, local health departments, and hospices. Nurses may be RNs, LVNs, or other types, with varied responsibilities based on their level of training.

When the nurse, doctor, or medical technician has extracted samples from a patient, the person who analyzes this is a laboratory tech. This individual uses machines that practically do all the testing and when the results come out it is up to him or her to analyze the results and submit the findings to the doctor.

Medical technicians who specialize in drawing blood from patients are called phlebotomists.

The doctor will decide what needs to be done to help the patient after reviewing the laboratory results. If the patient is bleeding internally, surgery may be required and a surgeon will have to be called in to remedy the situation. In cases where chemotherapy is needed, a technician who is trained in administering these treatments will be the one to kill cancer cells in the patient's body.

For patients that are injured and need time

to recover, a physical therapist or an occupational therapist will be there to help the person learn to use their arms, legs, and muscles once again. If the patient has suffered from a traumatic event, a specialist called a psychotherapist will try to help the patient. For those that have a difficult time speaking, a speech pathologist or speech therapist may help so the words that come out can easily be understood by others.

Obese patients may lose those extra pounds by working with a dietitian. This person will tell the patient what he or she should eat and those foods that should be avoided.

## The World of Dentistry

When you suffer with a toothache, a dentist is the health care provider to see. But for those that want to fix their teeth and make them straight, you will need to see an orthodontist. And a crew of trained dental assistants and dental hygienists support the work of the dentists.

## The World of Chiropractic

You may know someone who has a back problem and going to the doctor has not produced any positive results. If you become a chiropractor, you may be the answer to their prayers because this specialist may relieve the problem for good.

A chiropractor performs his or her "adjustment" sessions holistically without the use of any drugs or surgical treatments. To make their treatment more effective, they will advise the patient to make some lifestyle changes such as a change in diet, exercise, and sleeping habits.

There are times when the chiropractor will have to make a manual adjustment in the spinal column using water, light massage, electrical, heat, or ultrasound therapy. To make sure it lasts, they may apply braces, tapes, and straps.

## Career Medical Training

We start going to school at the age of 4 or 5. We graduate from high school at the age of 17 or

18. Those wanting to pursue a career as a doctor will have to endure 4 years of undergraduate studies, 4 years of medical school, 3 to 7 years as an intern and resident and then a couple of more years to move into a specialized field. This means that you will have only established yourself as a doctor after you have reached the age of 30!

Do you really have to wait that long to undergo medical training and make a career for yourself? The answer is no. This is because aside from being a doctor, you can do something else in the medical field. To give you an idea, here are some of them.

For those who don't want to work in a hospital, you can try to get a job as a pharmacist. This person is the one that dispenses prescription drugs at a pharmacy. They can also recommend a drug similar to what was prescribed if this is not available or is beyond your budget. Sometimes, they also help doctors determine proper dosages to be given to the patient as they are well aware of the side effects of giving too much to a patient.

Another job that you may apply for is that of a lab technician. These individuals, depending on their training, are the ones who test samples or man the X-ray or mammogram when a patient has to be examined.

One job that is high in demand right now in the US is that of nurse. This is because a lot of those who are working right now are nearing retirement age and fewer young people these days are entering the nursing profession, which is why nurses are being hired from other countries.

A career in the medical field will be challenging, but proportional to the amount of challenge are the benefits and satisfaction of securing a job in this career. For instance, the training and certification for being a medical coder will not only land a job as a medical encoder in the different types of healthcare and medical facilities such as medical clinics, hospitals, nursing homes, hospice programs, and outpatient facilities. But one can also decide to own their own medical coder business and earn more money by servicing different clientele through a successfully managed business.

This option will not only secure one's financial needs but will also allow one to choose and manage their own work schedules. That's certainly more than one can ever hope for in some other line of business or career.

Good opportunities abound for the medical coder. The same is true for almost all other types of career in the medical field. For instance, medical assistants can opt to take continuing education into the field of nursing. Once a medical assistant graduates into a career in nursing, the pay and incentives are considerably higher for them.

This is why the money and effort put into a medical college, trade school, or community college training program is time and money well spent. Not many other career options can offer the same privileges and guarantees. This is why, if you want to take advantage of this opportunity, you need to be on the lookout for a good medical training program to apply for.

Even if you already have a job and cannot afford to take the time off to go fulltime in building a career in medical college, don't despair. Most, if not all, medical colleges, trade schools, and community colleges offer courses during flexible times and online in order to allow individuals to take continuing education without having to quit their day jobs.

See Anything You Like?

The medical field has expanded tremendously through the years and the job descriptions mentioned here serve to show you the employment variety that is out there. Each of these jobs is different. If you want to become a nurse or doctor later on after working awhile at an entry level, it can be done with hard work.

These job descriptions have been an overview. The following chapters will go into greater detail about specific job areas. If you feel that any of these job descriptions for medical careers fits your interests and background then you may just decide to pursue a fulfilling livelihood in that area of healthcare.

Training for each of the jobs varies. For pharmacists, lab technicians, and nurses, you don't have to study for 8 years or more. You can qualify for a position after a couple of years in vocational school.

You will study subjects such as anatomy, biology, chemistry, infection control, medical terminology, physiology, and several others before undergoing hands-on training. There will be exams to test your knowledge of each subject so there won't be any problems when it is time to do the real thing.

You can also be successful working outside the hospital with a little medical training. You can get into medical transcription since all you have to do is transcribe what the doctor has said using a tape recorder. The work can be done at home and then the document is sent back to the doctor.

Another alternative will be to get into sales as pharmaceutical companies need sales agents to sell their drugs to doctors and hospitals.

Anyone can make a career once he or she has undergone medical training. You just have to decide what you want to specialize in and then go for it. For those that don't have the money to study full time, look for a school that offers this part time or online.

Remember, this is only temporary because once you earn your degree, you can make your career out of it.

Chapter Three

# Descriptions of Medical-Related Jobs

When you go to see a doctor, the first person that will greet you at the office is a medical assistant, whose job is to make sure that the office is running smoothly. They will tell you to wait for a while, and when to go in to the exam room or doctor's office if the doctor is busy attending to another patient. The medical assistant takes care of the paper work such as filing medical records and other duties that are handed down by the doctor.

Medical Assistant

Medical assistants play a vital role in the healthcare system as they serve and fulfill different administrative and clerical roles needed to support the services in various healthcare facilities. The job of the medical assistant is to take care of the details like bookkeeping, filling out and managing patient charts and files, arranging appointments, and sometimes performing basic in-house minor medical procedures like taking care of sutures and dressing bandages.

Medical assistants must have good communications skills and must be skilled enough in dealing with people to allow them to put patients at ease whether they are calling in by telephone or actually visiting the clinic.

While some medical assistants may move on to become nurses, many of them are happy and fulfilled to stay as medical assistants for their entire careers.

## Build a Career as a Medical Assistant

Many people are now considering building their career in the medical field. The medical field is one of the fastest growing sectors these days because of the great demand for excellent health care services. The country's economy and growth are dependent on good quality healthcare services. One promising option for individuals looking at opportunities in the medical field is a career as a medical assistant.

Demand for medical assistants are at an all-time high as more and more opportunities for quality healthcare outfits are popping up in response to the need of a growing population with specialized needs. A medical assistant will be able to find a job in a doctor's clinic, in outpatient services, in therapy clinics, and in other facilities providing healthcare.

If you are considering a job in the medical field, you may want to look into a career as a medical assistant. Below is some helpful information to help you find out more about this job, what it entails, and if this is the right choice for you.

Are you cut out to be a medical assistant?

If you have at least a high school diploma, possess a pleasant personality, can stay on top of multiple tasks, and can coordinate and organize well then you may just want to consider a career as a medical assistant. This is especially true for people who derive satisfaction from giving the proper health care and attention that each individual deserves.

It is important for medical assistants to be compassionate and caring, because they interface with patients and are often the first person that a patient sees upon entering a physician's clinic. This is why—coupled with warmth and compassion—medical assistants must also be good communicators. Aside from this, multiple responsibilities are required of a medical assistant, which is why one must be detail oriented, analytical, and love challenges.

If these criteria resonate with you, then a job as a medical assistant is right for you.

What does a medical assistant do?

A medical assistant is the caring face and may serve as the personality behind the atmosphere of a medical or healthcare facility. More specific to the medical assistant's job are administrative and clerical tasks.

It is the medical assistant who arranges appointments, fills out a patient's chart, and makes sure that these documents are properly filed for easy access and documentation. They also perform a variety of bookkeeping and front desk tasks.

Aside from these duties, a medical assistant may also perform basic in-house facility testing, changing wound dressings, administering injections, and such. This is why some medical assistants advance in their career by moving on to being a nurse. However, not all do this and many indeed choose to pursue being medical assistants for many years. This is because they find the job lucrative, stable, and fulfilling.

The job of a medical assistant is very important and, in fact, contributes to the level of success in the care of each patient. Because of the medical assistant's job, the doctor and other healthcare professionals are able to concentrate more on their jobs.

If so far you feel that a career as a medical assistant is indeed for you, the next step would be to check out learning institutions that offer training and mentoring for people who want to become medical assistants.

## Surgical Technologist

A surgical technologist or technician is a healthcare professional that assists a surgeon during operating room procedures. They perform various tasks during different phases of a surgical procedure. Before an operation, they prepare the operating room by assisting the surgical team, taking responsibility for the necessary items and supplies needed for surgery.

During the actual surgery, it is the surgical technologist or technician that passes equipment, supplies, and instruments needed to the surgeon. Aside from this, they may also prepare medications, deliver specimens to the lab, and assist with dressings and sutures. The work of the surgical technician doesn't end with the surgical procedure. After surgery, the surgical technologist makes sure that the equipment, instruments, and used materials are properly taken cared of to ensure the integrity of the sterile environment of the operating area for each incoming patient.

For the most part, surgical technologists can be found in the hospital setting — but they are not limited to this. Surgical technologists can choose to build careers in private medical offices with specific areas of specialization that suit their interests. For instance, they can choose private medical offices that focus on pediatrics, cardiology, physical therapy, plastic surgery, dental surgery, and many other specialties.

This job of surgical technician is well suited for individuals that can handle pressure and can think on their feet with the added bonus of not having to work in a regular 9 to 5 office setting.

Certified Nursing Assistant

As a certified nursing assistant, you'll be on the front lines of patient care. While "nursing

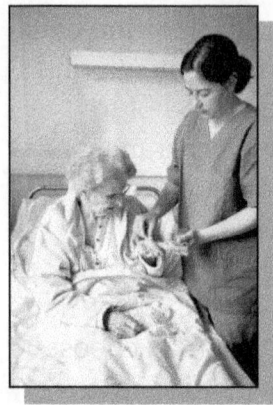 assistant" may not be the most glorified job title in a hospital, nursing care facility, or hospice setting, it's certainly one of the most vital to daily operations. Employment opportunities are plentiful. Your compassion and skill in patient care will help minimize the stress of those who are sick or unable to care for themselves.

Certified nursing assistants (CNAs), also known as nurses' aides, orderlies, patient care technicians, and home health aides, work under the supervision of a nurse to provide assistance to patients with daily living tasks.

Working closely with patients, CNAs are responsible for basic care services such as bathing, grooming and feeding patients, assisting nurses with medical equipment, and checking patient vital signs. CNAs give patients important social and emotional support and also provide vital information on patient conditions to nurses.

Many RNs start as CNAs. Being a CNA can be a stepping stone before becoming a registered nurse.

*Chapter Four*

# Dental Assistants

The U.S. Bureau of Labor Statistics' *Occupational Outlook Handbook, 2010-11 Edition* reports that job prospects for dental assistants should be excellent for years to come.

In this chapter you will see the following information relating to the work of Dental Assistants:

- Nature of the Work
- Training, Qualifications, and Job

Advancement
- Employment Opportunities
- Career Outlook
- Employment Projections
- Earnings
- Related Occupations

Significant Points to consider:

- Dentists are expected to hire more assistants to perform routine tasks so that dentists can devote their time to more complex procedures.

- Many assistants learn their skills on the job, although an increasing number are trained in dental-assisting programs; most programs take one year or less to complete.

- More than one-third of dental assistants work part time (2008).

## What Is the Nature of the Work?

Dental assistants perform a variety of patient care, office, and laboratory duties. They sterilize and disinfect instruments and equipment, prepare and lay out the instruments and materials required to treat each patient, and obtain and update patients' dental records. Assistants make patients comfortable in the dental chair and prepare them for treatment. During dental procedures, assistants work alongside the dentist to provide assistance. They hand instruments and materials to dentists and keep patients' mouths dry and clear by using suction hoses or other devices. They also instruct patients on postoperative and general oral healthcare.

Dental assistants may prepare materials for impressions and restorations, and process dental x rays as directed by a dentist. They also may remove sutures, apply topical anesthetics to gums or cavity-preventive agents to teeth, remove excess cement used in the filling process, and place dental dams to isolate teeth for treatment. Many States are expanding dental assistants' duties to include tasks such as coronal polishing and restorative dentistry functions for those assistants who meet specific training and experience requirements.

Dental assistants with laboratory duties make casts of the teeth and mouth from impressions, clean and polish removable appliances, and make temporary crowns. Those with office duties schedule and confirm appointments, receive patients, keep treatment records, send bills, receive payments, and order dental supplies and materials.

Dental assistants must work closely with, and under the supervision of, dentists. Additionally, dental assistants should not be confused with dental hygienists, who are licensed to perform a different set of clinical tasks.

## Work Environment

Dental assistants work in a well-lighted, clean environment. Their work area is usually near the dental chair so that they can arrange instruments, materials, and medication and hand them to the dentist when needed. Dental assistants must wear gloves, masks, eyewear, and protective clothing to protect themselves and their patients from infectious diseases. Assistants also follow safety procedures to minimize the risks associated with the use of x-ray machines.

Almost half of dental assistants had a 35- to 40-hour workweek in 2008. More than one-third worked part time, or less than 35 hours per week, and many others have variable schedules. Depending on the hours of the dental office where they work, assistants may have to work on Saturdays or evenings. Some dental assistants hold multiple jobs by working at dental offices that are open on different days or by scheduling their work at a second office around the hours they work at their primary office.

## Training, Qualifications, and Advancement

Many assistants learn their skills on the job, although an increasing number are trained in dental-assisting programs offered by community and junior colleges, trade schools, technical institutes, or the Armed Forces. Most programs take one year to complete. For assistants to perform more advanced functions, or to have the ability to complete radiological procedures, many States require assistants to obtain a license or certification.

## Education and training

In most States, there are no formal education or training requirements to become an entry-level dental assistant. High school students interested in a career as a dental assistant should take courses in biology, chemistry, health, and office practices. For those wishing to pursue further education, the Commission on Dental Accreditation (CODA) approved 281 dental-assisting training programs in 2009. Programs include classroom, laboratory, and preclinical instruction in dental-assisting skills and related theory. Most programs take close to one year to complete and lead to a certificate or diploma. Two-year programs offered in community and junior colleges lead to an associate degree. All programs require a high school diploma or its equivalent, and some require science or computer-related courses for admission. A number of private vocational schools offer 4- to 6-month courses in dental assisting, but the Commission on Dental Accreditation does not accredit these programs.

A large number of dental assistants learn through on-the-job training. In these situations, the employing dentist or other dental assistants in the dental office teach the new assistant dental terminology, the names of the instruments, how to perform daily duties, how to interact with patients, and other things necessary to help keep the dental office running smoothly. While some things can be picked up easily, it may be a few months before new dental assistants are completely knowledgeable about their duties and comfortable doing all their tasks without assistance.

A period of on-the-job training is often required even for those who have completed a dental-assisting program or have some previous experience. Different dentists may have their own styles of doing things that need to be learned before an assistant can be comfortable working with them. Office-specific information, such as where files and instruments are kept, will need to be learned at each new job. Also, as dental technology changes, dental assistants need to stay familiar with the instruments and procedures that they will be using or helping dentists to use. On-the-job training may be sufficient to keep assistants up-to-date on these matters.

### Licensing and Certification

Most States regulate the duties that dental assistants are allowed to perform. Some States require licensure or registration to perform expanded functions or to perform radiological procedures within a dentist's office. Licensure may include attending an accredited dental assisting program and passing a written or practical examination. Many States also require continuing education to maintain licensure or registration. However, a few States allow dental assistants to perform any function delegated to them by the dentist. Since requirements vary widely by State, it is recommended to contact the appropriate State board directly for specific requirements.

### The Certified Dental Assistant (CDA)

credential, administered by the Dental Assisting National Board (DANB), is recognized or required in more than 37 States toward meeting various requirements. Candidates may qualify to take the DANB certification examination by graduating from a CODA-accredited dental assisting education program or by having two years of full-time, or four years of part-time, experience as a dental assistant. In addition, applicants must have current certification in cardiopulmonary resuscitation. For annual recertification, individuals must earn continuing education credits. Other organizations offer registration, most often at the State level.

Individual States have also adopted different standards for dental assistants who perform certain advanced duties. In some States, dental assistants who perform radiological procedures must complete additional training distinct from that required to perform other expanded functions. Completion of the Radiation Health and Safety examination or the Certified Dental Assistant examination offered by Dental Assisting National Board (DANB) meets the standards in 30 States and the District of Columbia. Some States require completion of a State-approved course in radiology as well. Twelve States have no formal requirements to perform radiological procedures.

## Other Qualifications

Dental assistants must be a second pair of hands for a dentist; therefore, dentists look for people who are reliable, work well with others, and have good manual dexterity.

## Certification and Advancement

Without further education, advancement opportunities are limited. Some dental assistants become office managers, dental-assisting instructors, dental product sales representatives, or insurance claims processors for dental insurance companies. Others go back to school to become dental hygienists. For many, this entry-level occupation provides basic training and experience and serves as a steppingstone to more highly skilled and higher paying jobs. Assistants wishing to take on expanded functions or perform radiological procedures may choose to complete coursework in those functions allowed under State regulation or, if required, obtain a State-issued license.

## Employment Opportunities

Dental assistants held about 295,300 jobs in 2008. About 93 percent of all jobs for dental assistants were in offices of dentists. A small number of jobs were in the Federal, State, and local governments or in offices of physicians.

## Job Outlook

Employment is expected to increase much faster than average; job prospects are expected to be excellent.

### Employment change

Employment is expected to grow 36 percent from 2008 to 2018, which is much faster than the average for all occupations. In fact, dental assistants are expected to be among the fastest growing occupations over the 2008–18 projection period. Population growth, greater retention of natural teeth by middle-aged and older people, and an increased focus on preventative dental care for younger generations will fuel demand for dental services. Older dentists, who have been less likely to employ assistants or have employed fewer, are leaving the occupation and will be replaced by recent graduates, who are more likely to use one or more assistants. In addition, as dentists' workloads increase, they are expected to hire more assistants to perform routine tasks, so that they may devote their own time to more complex procedures.

## Job prospects

Job prospects should be excellent, as dentists continue to need the aid of qualified dental assistants. There will be many opportunities for entry-level positions, but some dentists prefer to hire experienced assistants, those who have completed a dental-assisting program, or have met State requirements to take on expanded functions within the office.

In addition to job openings due to employment growth, some job openings will arise out of the need to replace assistants who transfer to other occupations, retire, or leave for other reasons.

Employment, 2008 – 295,300

Projected Employment, 2018 — 400,900

## Earnings

Median annual wages of dental assistants were $32,380 in May 2008. The middle 50 percent earned between $26,980 and $38,960. The lowest

10 percent earned less than $22,270, and the highest 10 percent earned more than $46,150.

Benefits vary substantially by practice setting and may depend upon whether or not the dental assistant has full-time employment. According to a 2008 survey conducted by the Dental Assisting National Board (DANB), 86 percent of Certified Dental Assistants (CDA) reported receiving paid vacation from their employers, and more than half of CDAs received health benefits.

The above wage data are from the Occupational Employment Statistics (OES) survey program, unless otherwise noted. For the latest National, State, and local earnings data, visit the Bureau of Labor Statistics website (see the Information section at the back of this book).

Related Occupations

Besides Dental Assistants, other workers support various health practitioners, including:

- Dental hygienists

- Medical assistants

- Occupational therapist assistants and aides

- Pharmacy technicians and aides

- Physical therapist assistants and aides

- Surgical technologists

*Chapter Five*

# Office Jobs in Medical-Related Fields

## What Is Medical Billing & Coding?

Medical Billing school graduates are generally employed in a clinical setting. They have little to no contact with patients, so the job is more relaxed than most healthcare-related professions.

Medical Billers organize and code the treatment information recorded by doctors, preparing it for the facility's records and sending it to insurance companies and agencies such as Medicare for payment. This could include descriptions of symptoms, observations, treatment outcomes, and medical history. Their prime responsibility is coding the information so it is accurate and can be used by all who need that data.

Medical coding has never been hotter

Medical coding is an excellent career field within the healthcare industry. It offers a great future and career possibilities. Scores of people have made this their life long career path. Medical coders work closely with other health care providers, medical billers, and health information departments in hospitals to coordinate health care, insurance, and healthcare professionals' billing needs. Many in this highly respected field elect to get certified to add recognized credentials to their name, and with experience and additional training they could eventually start their own freelance and consulting services from a small office in their home.

What About Professional Certification?

Don't let the words "lack of experience" hold you back. Often it's not lack of experience, but rather lack of recognized certification that keeps qualified medical coders from landing the better jobs. Learn about recognized certification that you may already qualify for, based on your training or work experience in this field.

If your objective is to work for a medical office group practice, healthcare network, or hospital, then keep in mind that most employers prefer and often require national certification as a competency standard for their office or organization. The U.S. Department of Labor reports that the demand for medical coding professionals remains high.

Is Continuing Education Needed for a Career in Medical Coding?

Choosing medical coding as career can be ideal for many people because it is a lucrative way to make a living that does not come bundled with the usual stresses of a typical 9 to 5 job. In fact, choosing a medical coding career is choosing to make a living with flexible time and work from home benefits. The question remains though: is continuing education needed for a career in medical coding?

The simple answer to this is yes. In order to better your employment opportunities, it would be beneficial for you to acquire the training required to familiarize yourself with the different ins and outs of medical coding.

You need to be able to understand and to learn all there is to know about medical coding. This is because a medical encoder is in charge of assigning specific codes to different medical services and procedures to enable healthcare providers to bill their patients for services rendered. This is the reason why medical coders are in demand in the industry.

What Skills Do You Need?
Medical Billing Training and Education

Medical Billers can get their career started with a certificate program which, depending on the particular medical billing course being taken, can be completed in as little as 6 months. If desired, there are associate degree options which entail a longer 18 - 24 months of schooling but include a broader range of study. Students can take classes in a campus setting or pursue online medical billing degrees to fit into a busy schedule.

### Typical Subjects for Medical Billing & Coding Students

- Medical Terminology
- Anatomy
- Physiology
- Data Coding and Abstraction
- Database Management

If you have skills for organizing, and you enjoy administrative work, then learning medical coding will be easy for you. There are specialized courses and training available for individuals who want to learn the skills used in medical coding. However, not all of the available courses will give you the necessary certifications needed to advance your career in this field. It will, however, equip you with the knowledge to pass necessary examinations to enable you to be awarded certifications. You can acquire CD/DVD instruction on passing professional certification exams if you prefer home study. These courses are also available online.

You will find that going the extra mile and investing time and resources into continuing education for a medical coding career will take you far. After all, medical coders are needed by several institutions like hospitals, medical clinics, and offices. If you have the proper accreditation and certification for this job then more opportunities present themselves to you.

The American Academy of Professional Coders offers different types of certifications after individuals have passed their examinations. Each certification is nationally recognized and while you can still get a medical coding job without these certifications, your options for employment are limited. If you are serious about a career in medical coding, it is better to take the examinations and acquire these certifications.

Most specialized training that medical schools offer for individuals who choose a career in medical coding will prepare you to take the examinations provided by the American Academy of Professional Coders. For this reason alone, it is beneficial to acquire additional education.

The American Academy of Professional Coders offers Procedural Coder Certification to those who pass a particular examination for this. After passing the exam and being a Certified Procedural Coder, the individual can then be considered for various prestigious opportunities as a medical encoder in different professional healthcare facilities, offices, and clinics.

That type of certification is basic and, if one wishes, you can also take the other types of examinations offered by the American Academy of Professional Coders. They offer Specialty Credentials that will enable an individual to prove their current expertise, or you can even use this to jump start your medical coding career into a different type of specialization altogether.

It really is worthwhile to pursue the continuing education needed for a career in medical coding because not only will the proper certification allow for a wider range of employment options, it will also open the door for you to be able to have and manage your own medical coding company.

## Medical Billing

There are several other occupational titles within the medical coding field: Billing Specialist, Coding Specialist, medical collector, patient account representative, claims analyst, claims processor, electronic claims processor, reimbursement specialist, claims reviewer, claims assistant professional, and billing coordinator.

A successful billing specialist or claims examiner must know medical terminology and anatomy, proper form completion, and needs to possess basic computer skills. You need typing or keyboarding speed of at least 35 words per minute. Your work will involve you with patients, other office staff, medical personnel, and customer service personnel. A calm, cooperative, and courteous personality is important, because the people you will be in contact with will be either colleagues of yours or of the practice, or they could be patients, who are at stressful points in their lives.

## Where Would You Work?

Medical billers usually work in an office setting. Sometimes billers do not work where patients are being seen. You may find billing offices and services in large corporate buildings and small suburban offices, or in the doctor's office itself. Work hours are usually light, Monday through Friday, 40 hour work weeks. Overtime is often available, and sometimes mandatory. Working for an insurance company is more likely to require overnight or late hour shifts. Many billers and coders are able to work from home, either working for themselves, getting independent physicians as clients, or they may work for larger firms that provide them with their workload via electronic means.

Medical billing occupations continue to be the fastest growing opportunity in healthcare. Insurance companies and the government spend much time and money researching and controlling claims fraud, abusive practices, and medical necessity issues. For these reasons, insurance companies, hospitals, pharmacies, and other providers are hiring. Most companies and practices are looking for experience or appropriate schooling because of the legal ramifications of incorrect billing practices.

Medical billers are also able to work independently out of their homes. They can set up electronic billing through their home computers.

Positions are also available in doctor's offices, hospitals, pharmacies, nursing homes, rehabilitation centers, insurance companies, accounting officers, legal offices, hospice agencies, and consulting firms.

There are currently no set standards for educational requirements in these fields. However, more employers are looking for some formal training at an accredited vocational or career training school. These schools range in training time from nine months to two years. Any shorter training length is not recommended.

You can pursue employment with:

- Hospitals
- Insurance Carriers
- Physicians' Practices
- Entrepreneurship
- And More

These fields do not always require certification, but it is highly recommended. Several organizations sponsor certification exams. Several types of certifications are available for different specializations. Some certifications are fairly new, so it is best that you research your field to find the best one suited to your needs. It is also encouraging to know that advancement opportunities are unlimited, including moving up to office manager, supervisor, manager, and director of billing for examining departments, directors of coding, reimbursement departments, revenue cycles, and so on. These jobs have a pay scale ranging from $8-$10 an hour to start and up to $30-$40 an hour.

## Medical Billing Employment Figures

According to Labor Bureau statistics, about 170,000 billing and coding specialists were employed in 2010. About 40 percent of them worked in hospitals, while the rest were employed mainly by physicians, nursing care centers, outpatient facilities, and home health care services.

## Average Medical Coder Salaries (2006)

- At a Hospital Outpatient Clinic: $39,582
- As an Independent Contractor: $59,518
- At a Government Facility: $41,924
- At an Insurance Company: $43,843
- Multispecialty Group Medical Practice: $38,962
- Single Specialty Group Medical Practice: $36,912

- In a Physician Billing Service: $36,166
- Solo Medical Practice: $33,706

## The Career Outlook

The U.S. Labor Bureau predicts the number of Medical Billing school graduates getting jobs through the year 2016 will grow by 18 percent. One of the reasons for this increased demand is the growing number of medical tests and treatments performed by hospitals, clinics, and doctors. A heightened scrutiny of these procedures has created a priority need for accurate documentation in the medical field.

Recent federal legislation has also mandated that medical records be kept in electronic format, creating a demand for even more record-keeping personnel such as Medical Billing specialists.

See the resources section of this book for names and addresses of the organizations for medical billing specialists. It is recommended that you join at least one of them, but research them carefully to find the one that fits your career goals. Remember also that these organizations may have local chapters where you live, so check your local telephone directory.

www.highpayingmedicaljob.com
For more help see page 88

Finding the Right Billing & Coding Program

Not all Medical Billing & Coding schools are created equal. Their programs focus on varying combinations of ICD, CPT and HCPCS coding material, plus other factors such as program length and accreditation. The program you graduate from determines whether you're prepared to enter a hospital-based workplace, a physician-based environment, or another facet of the healthcare industry.

Whether you're preparing for AHIMA certification as a CCS or RHIT, or planning to take the AAPC's exam to become a CPC, enrolling in the right program is the key to the career you want. The way to choose the best school is to get information about each program's focus, then compare them side by side. You can then gauge which program is the right one for you, and plan your career accordingly.

This job is well suited for individuals that can work comfortably under pressure and can think on their feet. It offers the added bonus of not always having to work in a regular 9-5 office setting.

*Chapter Six*

# Medical Transcription

What Does a Transcriptionist Do?

The duties of a medical transcriptionist involve listening to a doctor's recorded notes and "typing" them into a predetermined format. A medical transcriptionist listens to the doctor's notes on a headset and types out the information, editing for clarity when necessary. As a medical transcriptionist you might prepare medical discharge orders, test results, autopsy reports, referral letters, consultation notes, and similar documents. This requires a good working knowledge of medical terminology and the ability to accurately convey information.

## What It Takes to be a Transcriptionist

Becoming a medical transcriptionist requires a two-year associate's degree or a one-year diploma from a medical transcriptionist training program. Familiarity with medical jargon is definitely a plus.

 These are traditionally office jobs; however, modern technology has made it possible for you to perform all of these tasks from home — telecommuting. More and more employers are realizing the many paybacks of allowing employees to work from home. Education and career training are available for the jobs that will enable your desire to work from the comfort of your own home.

A medical transcriptionist's job is to transcribe previously recorded patient data into a hard copy or a computer file. It isn't always possible for healthcare professionals to diligently fill out forms and charts of patient data, histories, and notes, so they first dictate a tape or digital recording of this and the medical transcriptionist reviews this voice recording and makes a proper file for use later on.

Naturally, it is very helpful for the medical transcriptionist if he or she has existing knowledge of anatomy and general physiology, as well as medical terminology to be able to do the job effectively.

## Pay Scale

Salary: In recent surveys, medical transcriptionists earned an average salary of $31,250 per year.

Medical transcription is for individuals looking to build a career in the medical field doing a task that allows for flexible schedules while being well compensated.

*Chapter Seven*

# Careers in medical sales

### Medical Device Careers

Sales agents who work for pharmaceutical companies not only sell drugs to doctors, they also sell devices such as pacemakers. The best part of being a sales agent is that you don't need a medical degree to get started. You simply have to know what you are selling and then making that pitch.

The first thing you have to do is apply for that position. That means polishing your resume and emailing or handing this out to potential medical device companies needing sales agents. If you have an interview coming up soon, you should do some research about the company and be familiar with their products so that if there is anything unclear, you can ask about this when it is your turn to raise questions during the interview.

It is also possible to ask your interviewer to do a SWOT analysis of their company because you will be able to understand what are their strengths, weaknesses, opportunities and threats.

As for the information about the potential employer, check out the corporate website. Don't forget to look at articles that have been written by various publications about them.

When the interview is over, ask how it went so you will have the opportunity to know what you need to improve on. This will also give you time to clear up anything that you may have missed earlier because this is the only way to show that even if you don't get hired, you won't make the same mistake when you are called by another company for an interview.

If, however, you are hired, then you should be familiar with the product. Most companies have product training programs which will you give time to learn about this device inside and out. This should also prepare you to answer any questions that potential buyers may have, like what makes your product different than that of the competitor.

Those who are able to sell their product will be able to make a lot of money in terms of sales commissions. Analysts have seen that selling medical devices is a very lucrative career as more machines are released each year.

But the medical device career does not end by just selling the product. If you have the talent and skill to make further improvements to the product you can apply to work as part of the research and development department of the company.

To do this, you have to keep in mind that what you are building must have high reliability and only minor problems during its life span. It should be something that doctors and nurses will be able to use.

This is done by what is known as reliability science, defined as the probability of a product performing without any glitches. If the odds of it faltering are quite low, then more hospitals will want to buy this machine.

Will you succeed in a career selling or making medical devices? That entirely falls upon you. If you have the skill or want to give it a shot, there is no harm trying. Should things not go your way, maybe you can still be in the medical field selling drugs, doing lab work in a research facility, or working with doctors by some other means.

## What Would You Sell?

Hospitals require a lot of medical equipment so their patients can be treated. They need monitors, respirators, beds, and computers, to name just a very few of their requirements. They also need printed forms, hypodermic syringes and needles, exam table covers, laundry services, furniture, thermometers, tongue depressors — and countless other supplies.

Somebody sells these things to hospitals, clinics, doctors, and other medical facilities. Given the fact that these facilities will need a lot of these items on a recurring basis, a good sales rep can make money earning tidy sales commissions from a career in selling medical equipment and supplies.

As a sales agent, your clients include not only new hospitals under construction but also existing hospitals, because they need to upgrade their facility's equipment from time to time and to resupply their expendable supplies. There are also private and public clinics, nursing homes, rehabilitation centers, hospice programs, and other facilities which you can visit and all you have to do is set up an appointment with whoever is in charge of their purchasing.

Whenever you meet with them, you show pictures and samples of your products. At times, you may even have to leave a few samples with them so they can try it out. To make your presentation look impressive, you can even create or have someone make a computer generated presentation.

Explaining the features and advantages of the medical equipment your company sells is just one aspect of the job. You should also be ready to answer questions that they may ask. For that, you should ask yourself, if you were a doctor (or nurse, or therapist…) what would you want to know about the product? Then practice how you will answer them by doing mock up sales presentations.

How do you know if the purchasing agent will buy the medical equipment you have or if they will tell you they are not interested? The best indicator is how they respond both verbally and non-verbally. If they express interest by asking how many do you have or when this can be delivered, you know you have made a sale. Another indicator is if they have a smile on their face or nod their head affirmingly.

Once you see these signals, it is time to close the deal. You can ask directly how many do they want and then tell them when these will be delivered. It also wouldn't hurt to throw in some freebies to the deal so they know they are getting a good bargain buying the medical equipment from you instead of a competitor.

If they are not ready to make a decision, give them some time to think about it and then visit or call again a few days later. You have to remember that medical equipment costs a lot of money even if they buy just one or two and they will probably have to review their budget.

Whatever happens, remember to thank them for their time in seeing you. Who knows, they may not be interested in getting medical equipment from you now but if they are not happy with what they purchased from a competitor, they may decide to go back to you in the future.

If they buy from you, be sure to follow up on how the equipment is doing. This will give you the chance to check if they are satisfied with your product and if they are interested in buying more or something else in your catalog. Always thank a customer for buying from you. Write them a personal note or drop off an appropriate gift (flowers, a handsome writing instrument...).

Hospitals need medical equipment and pharmaceuticals to treat patients. By doing your job as a sales agent, you contribute to the patients' comfort when they have to undergo surgery or have to be confined there for a few days.

## Medical Sales Opportunities Abound

The high demand for individuals to fill jobs in the medical field is not simply brought about by new job opportunities. The demand is actually fueled by the need for excellent health care services needed by a growing and prospering population. Truth of the matter is, there are no new career offerings in the medical field. There are just more opportunities available now for well-established jobs in the medical field and one such example is medical supply sales.

## Durable Medical Equipment

Medical supply sales careers are not a new thing. In fact, these jobs have been around for a long time. The most common type of medical supply sales job is that of the medical equipment representative.

These days, though, sales careers in medicine are not confined to sales reps from different pharmaceutical companies trying to sell different prescription and non-prescription drugs to physicians. Medical supply sales careers are more encompassing than that these days, as different outfits need more and more individuals to join their workforce to help push the trial and sales of different medical supplies to health care facilities.

Medical supply sales careers are now not only offered by pharmaceutical companies but by different medical and health care companies that have good products to sell through targeted sales tactics.

*Chapter Eight*

# Pharmaceutical Sales

A medical sales representative may be employed by a pharmaceutical company and it is this sales rep's job to call on physicians and to give them free samples of the drugs that the pharmaceutical company creates. Pharmaceutical sales representatives are employed by pharmaceutical companies to deliver targeted marketing to physicians who have the power to prescribe these medications to their patients. This way, pharmaceutical companies can push the sales of their products through the doctors that prescribe them to the patients that need them. Sales persons in this field should possess some background in biology or other associated disciplines. However, pharmaceutical employers will train sales representatives on the contents of their product lines.

This type of sales tactic is especially successful for marketing and pushing the sales of prescription drugs. This is because mass marketing of prescription drugs is not possible and the best way to push sales is by targeting the physicians that can choose to prescribe them to their patients.

Getting into this type of job is especially promising, lucrative, and satisfying for those who have an inclination for sales. If you don't have any sales experience, or you're not sure if a career in sales is for you, don't despair. A medical supply sales career may still be for you.

Needed Skills

Sales people possess excellent communications skills focused on the ability to persuade and convince others into a desired action. In the case of the medical representative of a pharmaceutical company, the sales person needs to convince the physician to choose their type of medication over the rest. To do this, the sales rep needs very good relationship-building and management skills. Most medicines in the same category have the same attributes and efficacy, so sometimes it really all boils down to the skill of the medical rep to sell his products effectively.

Given this, particularly good medical sales reps are compensated very well through actual financial perks and fringe benefits like a good company car and vacation and leisure packages. This is why many people consider getting into this type of job and decide to stay and advance in their careers here.

*Chapter Nine*

# Pharmacy Technician

A pharmacy technician assists a licensed pharmacist fill prescriptions. Qualified pharmacy techs need to know more than just how to count pills or bottles.  As their role expands, career opportunities for pharmacy technicians increase, and the outlook for employment in this field is strong. Now is an excellent time to become a pharmacy technician. This is a solid health care career.

There is a push toward online pharmacy technician training. Some people still prefer to learn in a classroom setting, but online training courses provide a great deal of freedom for students needing to keep a flexible schedule due to other work or family responsibilities. Online pharmacy technician courses teach you the same information and give you the same degree as classroom programs; however, online study lets you learn at your own pace. If you are already familiar with a particular topic, you can cruise quickly through that material. On the other hand, if you have difficulty grasping a topic, you can focus on it as much as you need to until you master it. All reputable online pharmacy technician schools have instructors available by telephone and email to answer your questions. Even though you're learning on your own, you are not alone in the program.

What You'll Study in Pharmacy Technician Courses

Online pharmacy technician courses are usually distributed in sections or "modules." At the end of a module, you may be given an exam. When you pass the exam, the next module is sent to you electronically. If a program is labeled "distance learning," you may correspond with your school by mail as well as email. In some cases, you may need to attend certain classes that the school conducts either at their main campus or another convenient location. Topics that may be included in distance and online pharmacy technician courses include Medical Terminology, Pharmaceutical Calculations and Measurements, Label and Prescription Information, Anatomy/Physiology, and Poison/Drug Emergencies. Even if you do not have experience working with computers, online pharmacy technician courses make it easy to learn online. You would cover these same subjects in a trade school or community college setting.

## Why Get Certified as a Pharmacy Technician?

The pharmaceutical industry constantly searches for better medications and advancements in technology. The industry will always need skilled certified pharmacy technicians who desire to stay current on the latest medical innovations. Having your pharmacy technician certification means that you have passed the certification test given by the Pharmacy Technician Certification Board (PTCB,) and you have the basic knowledge to work as a pharmacy technician professional. Only a few states require you to be certified, but that list is growing as pharmacists depend more on technicians for support. Regardless of your state's regulations, you'll find that more and more employers are requiring pharmacy tech certification. Most pharmacy technician job postings say that they want candidates who are either already certified or are currently enrolled in pharmacy technician school.

## Certification Requirements

The prerequisites for taking the pharmacy technician certification exam are simple. You must have a high school diploma, GED, or foreign equivalent, and you must have no felony or drug-related convictions. Additionally, you must not be under any restrictions from any State Board of Pharmacy. If you meet the eligibility require-ments, you simply have to pass the pharmacy technician certification test administered by the PTCB. In order to keep your pharmacy technician certification status, you must complete 20 hours of continuing education every two years. At least one of those hours must be in pharmacy law.

The certification test is administered on a computer and consists of 90 multiple choice questions covering Assisting pharmacists in serving patients, Maintaining medication and inventory control systems, and Participating in the administration and management of pharmacy practice. There are testing sites around the country, and the test is offered year-round. Be prepared to pay a registration fee. Visit the Pharmacy Technician Certification Board website for more information. You will receive your official score by mail. If you do not pass, you may take the exam as many times as needed until you earn a passing score. The exam fee is required each time you take the exam. Once you pass the exam, you will have earned the designation of Certified Pharmacy Technician (CPhT).

Pharmacy Technician Salaries

As a new pharmacy tech, you'll start with an entry-level salary--this is typical of virtually any field. The good news about pharmacy technician salaries is that they have the potential to increase dramatically as you gain experience.

Salary Range (as reported by Salary.com)

Entry level Pharmacy Technicians with up to three years of experience can earn from $27,117 to $36,743 annually. A Pharmacy Tech with four or more years of experience can earn from $31,534 to $42,956 yearly. With six or more years of experience, he or she can move up to a Pharmacy Technician Supervisor earning between $41,306 and $59,518.

Factors Affecting Pharmacy Technician Salaries

Factors that play a role in determining a pharmacy tech's salary:

- More education level may make you a more attractive job candidate, quicken your advancement, and therefore boost your salary;
- Certification as a pharmacy tech may count more than educational level in qualifying you for a higher salary because it assures employers that your skills meet high standards in the field;
- Geographic location plays a part in determining salary, due to the local

economy and the cost of living in your area;
- The type of employer affects salary because a hospital or a large retail chain is often able to pay larger salaries than smaller independent pharmacies.

## Pharmacy Technician Benefits

Full-time pharmacy technicians generally receive some or all of the following benefits: Paid vacation, Paid holidays, Paid sick leave, 401(k) retirement plan, and Health benefits. Employers often reimburse continuing education tuition, so you can maintain your pharmacy technician certification status for free. When combined with base pay, these benefits can add up to an attractive compensation package.

*Chapter Ten*

# Medical Imaging Careers

Medical imaging technology is a vital tool in today's healthcare system, and workers with the skills to perform diagnostic imaging procedures are in high demand. You will find a wide variety of job opportunities in medical imaging, along with plenty of avenues for specializing in different technologies. Medical imaging requires a command of complex medical equipment, an understanding of the subject, and the type of image necessary for proper diagnosis. Medical imaging specialties include sonography / ultrasound and radiologic technology. In selecting a training institution, remember that school accreditation is an important indicator that a school meets high standards and will prepare you to meet the challenges of your chosen profession. Learn which accrediting bodies to look for as you search for schools. Find professional organizations that can help you on your medical imaging career path. There are several ways to finance your medical imaging education. Scholarships and financial aid grants are available through the federal government.

## Medical Imaging Glossary

"Medical Imaging" refers to a broad array of specialties. Below are several short definitions of different job titles and the basics about each of these various medical imaging careers:

## Radiologic Technologist

Radiologic technologists produce digital images of the body to help physicians diagnose their patients. The radiology tech,

also referred to as an X-ray tech, works with patients throughout their X-ray exams, coaching and positioning for optimal results.

## Ultrasound Techs

An ultrasound technician uses high frequency sound waves to create images of a patient's internal organs, blood flow within arteries, developing fetus, or other systems. Ultrasound imaging is gaining in popularity, and so careers in this field are growing. Ultrasound tech schools will help prepare you for a medical career as an ultrasound technologist. Ultrasound imaging, also called sonography, is used for making real-time, moving images of internal organs. Ultrasound technicians aid in diagnosing organ abnormalities and monitoring pregnancies.

## Ultrasound Technologist Salaries

Ultrasound technology includes the diagnosis of internal body disorders. These technicians may work in hospitals, clinics, research facilities, or in a doctor's private medical practice. The technician must have proper training, credentials, and work experience. Salaries for these technicians are not a well-defined figure, depending upon the locale where they are working, their level of experience, their qualifications, and the accreditations they have earned. Incomes can be very good for those who have outstanding qualifications. Experts expect his field to grow at the rate of 18 percent in the upcoming five to eight years.

The average salary of sonographers is around $60,000 annually. Advanced training and skills could increase this further--up to $80,000 per year or more. The type of employer has a major effect on pay scales. Private and public sector health care units offer widely differing pay scales to these professionals. Technicians working in hospitals or physician's offices can earn $67,000 annually and above, and those in the educational or research sectors will earn around $66,000. Sonographers working in outpatient settings have an average salary that is estimated to be around $64,000.

Salaries vary around the U.S. In some states, demand for this profession is high and so is the pay. On the other hand, however, some states are saturated with sonographers and pay is depressed. Work experience also matters, and

newly employed technicians will earn less initially, though later on they will earn more as experience and skill grow. Additional credentials from the ARDMS will increase demand for a sonographer's services in hospitals and other healthcare units. Specialization also enhances salary possibilities.

Summarizing, we can say that normally the salary of the ultrasound technician ranges between $45,000 to $66,000 and above. According to the overall data, beginning earnings for sonogram technicians start around $40,000, increasing up to $65,000 on the lower ranges and reaching $85,000 and above in the upper ranges. When figured as an hourly wage, pay ranges between $17.00 and $36.00 per hour. Overtime can boost hourly pay up to $20.00 to $54.00 per hour.

According to *Salary.com*, medical imaging salaries for the middle 50 percent of ultrasound technologists is between $59,349 and $70,862. The top 10 percent of ultrasound technologists make $76,336 or more. These pay scales, like others in this book, are for informational purposes only. Situations will vary from state to state, and from situation to situation.

## Medical Imaging Salaries

"Medical imaging" is a broad category that holds a number of different yet related professions. So when you're looking for information about medical imaging salaries — and more specifically, what you can expect to earn in a medical imaging career — it's important to know what kinds of careers are out there, and which one interests you.

## Radiologic Technologists Salaries

According to March 2010 data on Salary.com, radiologic technologists earn from $43,950 to $56,514. The U.S. Bureau of Labor Statistics reports that radiologic technologists earned between $43,510 and $64,070 in 2009.

## Typical Salary for a Radiology Tech

- Medical and diagnostic laboratories  –  $57,250
- General medical and surgical hospitals – $54,770
- Physicians' offices        –      $50,860

## Cardiovascular Technologists Salaries

According to the Bureau of Labor Statistics, medical imaging salaries for entry-level cardiovascular technologists are usually between $36,000 and $48,000. With more experience, however, the salary range increases to the level of between $60,000 and $75,000.

## Nuclear Medicine Technologists Salaries

Salary.com reports that medical imaging salaries for nuclear medicine technologists are between $62,743 and $$80,098.

## Radiation Therapist Salaries

Salary.com reported in March 2010 that radiation therapy technologists earn between $64,444 and $83,298.

## Related Careers

The following careers may not be standard medical imaging jobs; however, they are closely tied to the medical imaging field:

Cardiovascular Technologist — A cardiovascular technologist participates in medical procedures to diagnose and treat heart problems, including medical imaging techniques. A Radiation Therapist, instead of creating images, works with radiologists and oncologists to treat patients. While these professionals are certified by the same organizations as radiologic technicians, they use radiation technology in a very different way. Within the radiologic technologist career, there are opportunities to specialize, such as Computed Tomography (CT), Magnetic Resonance Imaging (MRI), mammography, and cardiac- and vascular-interventional radiography.

Radiologic Technology Jobs and Career Outlook

Before you get your radiologic technologist training, it's important to gather facts about the industry. You'll want to understand what radiology jobs are like and what the employment outlook is for the future. What is the difference between a radiology technician, a radiologic technologist, and a radiologist? Find out about the various job titles and career paths in radiology. Learn what each job entails and how it differs from other radiology jobs. Before you start your career as a radiologic technologist, it's important to learn about the certification requirements in your area. However, even if your state does not require certification, it can still be a good idea in terms of career advancement.

# For More Information

*The items listed below are provided by other sources and not by the author of this book. They provide in-depth information relating to the subject. Each listing describes the product, provides a full-length Internet address plus a "shorthand" bit-ly Internet address, and a QR Code which allows your smart phone to scan it and take you directly to that website.*

## Learn The Secrets Of Acing Your Next Medical Sales Interview and Landing Your Dream Job!!!

### You Will Learn How To:
Use Existing Relationships to Leverage Target Companies.
Uncover Medical Sales Jobs that are NOT Advertised.
Write a Resume that will "Get Your Foot in the Door."

www.highpayingmedicaljob.com
For more help see page 88

Write an Effective 30-60-90 Day Plan.
Sell Yourself During Medical Sales Interviews.
Learn to Ace Situation Interview Questions Like The Gallup.
WIN The Job – Beat Out Your Competition!

**Get 3 <u>FREE</u> resume templates**

http://bit.ly/oTLeGr

---

## After Reading This Jam-Packed 107 Page Manual You'll Know if a Home-Based Medical Billing Business is for You!

**Can this business really be started without any prior experience in this field?**

Exactly how much money must you invest into starting this home based business?

**What is the average home based medical biller salary, and what can you do to ensure that the amount continuously increases?**

Learn the how's and why's about the entire process and how to do it properly from home as a successful business venture.

**You get valid examples of contracts, marketing fliers, and other business forms that you will need to be familiar**

with.

Learn which three very important services you should be offering to prospective physicians.

**Find out what HIPAA is and why it impacts you and your business.**

Learn what you must do to get physicians for your new business and where to find their contact information.

**Know how to successfully market your business and services.**

Learn exactly what to say to prospective physicians and their staff to secure them as your client.

**See what forms you will need and where to go to download or buy them.**

Most importantly, you'll be able to decide based on facts if starting this service is the right business for you!

**And Much Much More!**

$29.00

http://bit.ly/nsIC42

---

## Medical Transcription A to Z

*Medical Transcription A to Z: A Comprehensive Guide and Workbook.* Here is your Secret Weapon that Reveals How to Get Started in this Versatile and Lucrative Home-Based Business, the Nuts and Bolts of Transcription, and How to Work at Home and Make Enough Money to Pay the Bills!

$27.00

http://bit.ly/nmFyoW

---

## How to Build A Million Dollar Medical Transportation Company

Guaranteed revenue! Leverage two of the world's largest and fastest growing niche markets – the elderly population and the medical industry. Despite our poor economy, the future of the medical transportation industry is booming with growth & opportunity. Invest in your future today.

$197.95

http://bit.ly/nWFrUQ

## These Videos Will Help You Pass the CPC Exam

**When you have completed your medical coding training, you have big plans to make a career in the medical coding field. Smart move! Your next step is to take either the Certified Professional Coder (CPC) exam or the Certified Coding Specialist-Physician Based (CCS-P) exam.**

**Here's what's great about these videos:**
They prepare you to **pass** the certification exam **ON THE FIRST TRY**
Teach you a proprietary **"Bubble and Highlighting Technique"** to help you use your manuals during the test — and afterwards during your daily coding work
Watching the dvds and online videos is **cheaper** than the live event I do twice a year
They help you be more confident about passing the CPC exam
You can fit watching the videos into y**our own schedule**
Easier to digest/take in the information on video than it is at a live event
You can pause the videos
You can **rewatch** the videos in the areas you need to work on
If it's a medical coding area that you feel comfortable with, you can skip it and **save time studying**
You can spend more time **studying problem areas**
My Blitz videos are the **only CPC exam preparation video system available on the internet**!

www.highpayingmedicaljob.com
For more help see page 88

You can **get started NOW** with the online videos!

$240.00

http://bit.ly/pOzfhh

---

# Associations and Professional Societies

Alliance of Claims Assistance Professionals (ACAP)
25500 Hawthorne Blvd #1158
Torrance, CA 90505
http://www.claims.org/
E-mail: capinfo@claims.org

## American Academy of Professional Coders (AAPC)
2480 South 3850 West, Suite B
Salt Lake City, UT 84120
800/626-CODE
http://www.aapc.com/
E-mail: info@aapc.com

Certification and extensive information for Coders, Office Managers, Claims Examiners, Hospital Outpatient Coders, Experienced Reimbursement Specialists and Coding Educators.

## American Association for Medical Transcription (AAMT)
100 Sycamore Avenue, Suite M
Modesto, CA 95354
800/982-2182
http://www.aamt.org

This website lists career information, employment opportunities, networking, local associations, and approved education programs. You can post your résumé online and receive e-mail job alerts.

## American Dental Assistants Association
35 East Wacker Dr., Suite 1730

Chicago, IL 60601
Internet: http://www.dentalassistant.org

For more information on a career as a dental assistant and for general information about continuing education in this field, contact the ADAA at the address above.

American Medical Billing Association (AMBA)
4297 Forrest Drive
Sulphur, OK 73086
580/622-2624
http://www.ambanet.net/AMBA.htm

The web site presents information about online courses, networking opportunities, and information on preparing for the examination to become a Certified Medical Reimbursement Specialist.

Commission on Dental Accreditation
American Dental Association
211 East Chicago Ave., Suite 1900
Chicago, IL 60611.
Internet: http://www.ada.org/117.aspx

Get information about career opportunities and accredited dental assistant programs is available from the ADA.

Dental Assisting National Board, Inc.
444 N. Michigan Ave., Suite 900
Chicago, IL 60611
Internet: http://www.danb.org

For information on becoming a Certified Dental Assistant
and for a list of State boards of dentistry, contact the above
organization.

Healthcare Information and Management Systems
Society (HIMSS)
230 East Ohio, Suite 500
Chicago, IL 60611-3269
312/664-4467
http://www.himss.org
E-mail: himss@himss.org

Includes a membership directory, résumé posting, job alerts, and
you can research potential employers and Career Development
Resources with résumé and interviewing advice (members only).

Health Professions Institute (HPI)
PO Box 801
Modesto, CA 95355-0801
209/551-2112

http://www.hpisum.com/
E-mail: hpi@hpisum.com

Publishes books, periodicals, and conducts seminars for the medical transcription community. They have a free Student Network and information on medical transcription courses. *Perspectives* magazine (an e-zine) is free to medical transcription professionals.

## Medical Coding and Billing
http://www.medicalcodingandbilling.com

This website presents information about coding and billing careers, including certification, education, and also medical office management career information. Lists of professional associations.

## Medical Group Management Association (MGMA)
104 Inverness Terrace East
Englewood, CO 80012
303/799-1111 or 877/275-6462
http://www.mgma.com

This organization is for the supervisors of medical group practices. The web site has job ads, networking, internship information, and a "Core Learning Series" for education. Job ads are in monthly a publication *MGMA Connections*.

Medical Records Institute
425 Boylston Street, 4th Floor
Boston, MA 02116
617/964-3923
http://www.medrecinst.com/index.shtml
E-mail: cust_service@medrecinst.com

This organization promotes electronic health records, mobile health, and related applications.

MT Jobs
http://www.mtjobs.com/

Sponsored by MT Daily, this site provides free job searches, résumé posting, e-mail job alerts, and employer profiles.

National Healthcareer Association (NHA)
134 Evergreen Place, 9th Floor
East Orange, NJ 07018
800/499-9092 or 973/678-9100
http://www.nha2000.com/

The National Healthcareer Association (NHA) offers education and certification for many health care jobs, including Certified Medical Trans-criptionist (CMT) and Certified Billing and Coding Specialist (CBCS).

Professional Association of Health Care Office Managers (PAHCOM)
461 East Ten Mile Road
Pensacola, FL 32534-9714
800/451-9311
http://www.pahcom.com/

Web site has information on education, local chapters, and on the Certified Medical Manager exam. The Benefits page of the web site posts job openings.

U.S. Bureau of Labor Statistics
Office of Occupational Statistics and Employment Projections
PSB Suite 2135
2 Massachusetts Avenue, NE
Washington, DC 20212-0001
http://www.bls.gov/OCO
Telephone: 1-202-691-5700

www.highpayingmedicaljob.com
For more help see page 88
100